Cornerstones of Freedom

The Assassination of Abraham Lincoln

BRENDAN JANUARY

CHILDREN'S PRESS®
A Division of Grolier Publishing
New York • London • Hong Kong • Sydney
Danbury, Connecticut

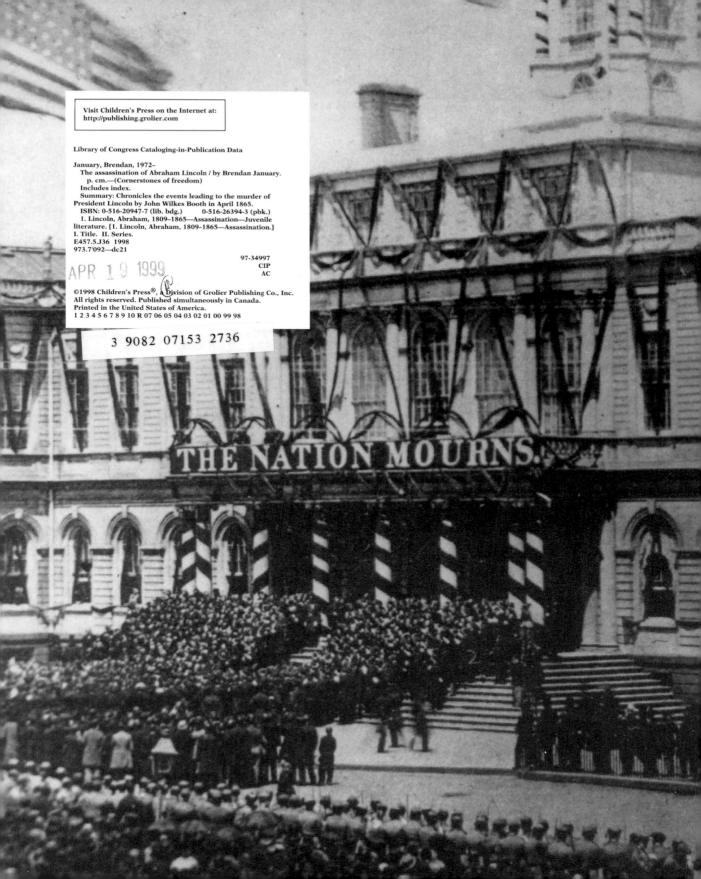

Visit Children's Press on the Internet at:
http://publishing.grolier.com

Library of Congress Cataloging-in-Publication Data

January, Brendan, 1972–
 The assassination of Abraham Lincoln / by Brendan January.
  p. cm.—(Cornerstones of freedom)
 Includes index.
 Summary: Chronicles the events leading to the murder of
President Lincoln by John Wilkes Booth in April 1865.
 ISBN: 0-516-20947-7 (lib. bdg.)   0-516-26394-3 (pbk.)
 1. Lincoln, Abraham, 1809–1865—Assassination—Juvenile
literature. [1. Lincoln, Abraham, 1809–1865—Assassination.]
I. Title. II. Series.
E457.5.J36 1998
973.7'092—dc21
                                    97-34997
                                         CIP
                                          AC

©1998 Children's Press®, a Division of Grolier Publishing Co., Inc.
All rights reserved. Published simultaneously in Canada.
Printed in the United States of America.
1 2 3 4 5 6 7 8 9 10 R 07 06 05 04 03 02 01 00 99 98

THE NATION MOURNS.

In 1860, the people of the United States anxiously awaited the outcome of the November presidential election. For years, the country had been divided over the issue of slavery, and many voters believed its future depended on which candidate became president. One of the candidates, Abraham Lincoln, promised to prevent the expansion of slavery into states and territories outside the South. This angered the people of the southern states, where slavery was considered vital to the economy. Many southerners vowed to secede from, or leave, the Union if Lincoln became president.

This photograph of Abraham Lincoln is the one that is used on the United States's $5 bill.

When Lincoln won the election, the southerners kept their promise. South Carolina seceded in December, followed by Georgia, Alabama, Florida, Mississippi, and Louisiana. In February 1861, the southern states formed the Confederate States of America. On April 12, 1861, the Confederates attacked Fort Sumter in South Carolina. Lincoln called for a volunteer army to crush the South's rebellion. The American Civil War had begun.

The war's cost to the nation was enormous. Hundreds of thousands of soldiers were tragically wounded or killed in battle. In the South, once-proud cities were reduced to piles of rubble and charred remains. Factories lay in ruins, and farm fields were choked with weeds.

President Lincoln struggled to save the Union. For four long years he suffered through costly victories and bitter defeats. Finally, on April 9, 1865, Lincoln heard good news. The Confederate army commanded by General Robert E. Lee had surrendered at Appomattox Court House, in Virginia. With the end of the war in sight, wild celebrations filled the streets of northern cities.

For some people, however, the war's end caused bitterness and desperation. John Wilkes Booth,

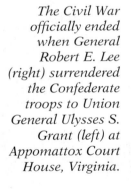

The Civil War officially ended when General Robert E. Lee (right) surrendered the Confederate troops to Union General Ulysses S. Grant (left) at Appomattox Court House, Virginia.

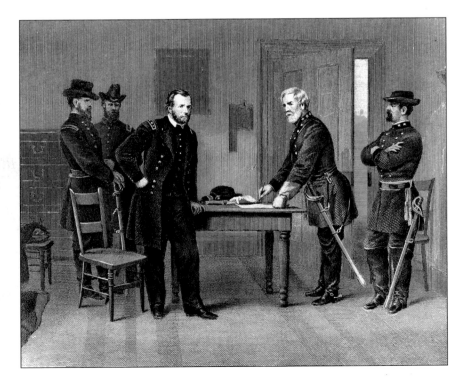

a young and handsome actor, was fiercely loyal to the Confederacy. He saw Lincoln as a tyrant who had waged a cruel war on the southern people. Booth later wrote in his diary: "Our country owed all her troubles to [Lincoln]."

In February 1865, Booth had plotted to kidnap President Lincoln. Booth hoped to exchange the captured president for thousands of Confederate soldiers who were being held in Northern prisons. On March 17, Booth and several companions crouched next to a road, hoping to ambush the president as he rode by. But Lincoln changed his planned route and he never appeared. As Booth waited for another opportunity to carry out his scheme, the Confederacy crumbled. By April 1865, Booth abandoned his plot to kidnap Lincoln. He wrote in his diary, "Our cause almost being lost, something great and decisive must be done." Booth felt convinced that the South could be saved if Lincoln was assassinated. He began looking for an opportunity to carry out the deed.

John Wilkes Booth was a well-known actor whose father and brother were also famous stars of the theater.

Although Booth kept a detailed diary, he did not pay attention to the dates at the top of the pages. This entry was actually written on April 14, 1865.

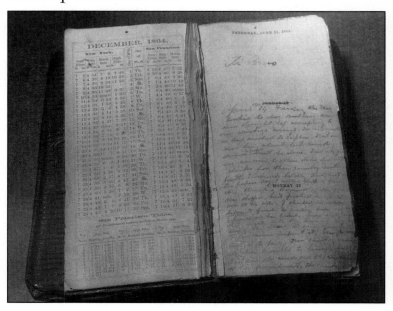

President Lincoln knew that he had many enemies. Several letters containing threats to end his life had arrived at the White House in Washington, D.C. Lincoln ignored them. If someone seriously intended to murder him, Lincoln claimed, he could do little to prevent it. Lincoln's advisors didn't agree. They begged him to travel with bodyguards. Lincoln permitted one guard, but not more.

Mary Todd Lincoln, in the gown she wore for her husband's first presidential inauguration, on March 4, 1861

Despite Lincoln's confident attitude, he was disturbed by a strange dream. On Tuesday, April 11, 1865, he discussed it with his wife Mary, and a few friends. Lincoln had dreamed that he was awakened by the sounds of sobbing. Puzzled, Lincoln rose from his bed and went downstairs, where the sounds of weeping grew louder. He wandered through several empty rooms. Finally, Lincoln entered the East Room of the White House and discovered a coffin surrounded by people dressed in black. "Who is dead?" Lincoln asked. "The president," replied a soldier. "He was killed by an assassin."

No one spoke after the president finished. Finally Mary said, "That is horrid. I wish you had

6

not told it." Lincoln tried to calm her fears. "It is only a dream," he explained. "Let us say no more about it, and try to forget it."

At breakfast on Friday, April 14, Mary reminded the president that they had tickets for a play called *Our American Cousin*. The comedy was being presented that evening in Ford's Theatre. During the past few years, Lincoln had enjoyed several plays at Ford's Theatre. Often, a good play helped him to forget his worries about the Civil War for a few hours. The Lincolns invited Ulysses S. Grant, the victorious Union general, to come along.

While the president and his wife made their theater plans, John Wilkes Booth strolled over to Ford's Theatre to pick up his mail. Booth regularly visited the theater, where he had acted several times on the stage. Booth soon learned that Lincoln planned to view a play that evening. He left the theater in great excitement and spent the next few hours in feverish preparation. He rented a fast horse and returned to his hotel room. There, he dressed in black clothes. Tucked in the pockets of his coat were a compass, a derringer pistol, and a knife.

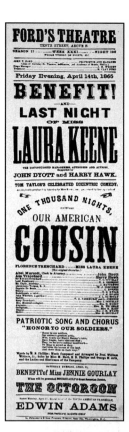

The playbill, or advertisement, for Our American Cousin *dated April 14, 1865, the night the Lincolns were in the audience.*

John Wilkes Booth checked in to the National Hotel in Washington, D.C., on April 8, 1865, and signed the hotel guestbook.

Lewis Paine

George Atzerodt

The peephole Booth drilled in the second door was about the size of a dime.

At about 2:30 P.M., Booth met with a companion, Lewis Paine. Tall and well-built, Paine was extremely strong and fierce. Booth told Paine about his plan. While Booth shot the president, Paine would attack and murder General Grant. Another companion, George Atzerodt, would assassinate Vice President Andrew Johnson. Booth hoped that murdering both the president and the vice president would cripple the United States government. In the confusion and panic, the Confederacy could turn defeat into victory. Booth dreamed that he would be hailed throughout the South as a hero.

Sometime during the afternoon hours, Booth returned to Ford's Theatre and made his final preparations for the assassination. The president, his wife, and General and Mrs. Grant would sit in a private theater box above the stage. A short narrow passageway, with doors on both ends, led to the box. Booth opened the first door and entered the passageway. He took a short wooden bar and laid it on the floor behind the door. That evening, Booth would jam it between the door and the wall, blocking the entrance to the passageway. This would prevent anyone in the audience from interfering. He then examined the second door that led directly into the private box. Using a hand drill, Booth carefully drilled a small peephole into the wooden door. Through the hole, he would clearly see where the president was seated.

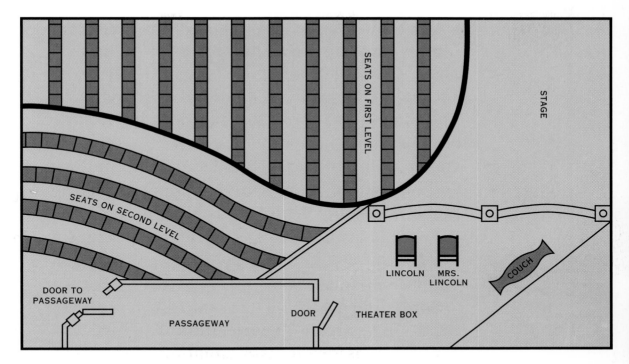

Within the illustration:

SEATS ON FIRST LEVEL

STAGE

SEATS ON SECOND LEVEL

LINCOLN   MRS. LINCOLN

COUCH

DOOR TO PASSAGEWAY

PASSAGEWAY   DOOR   THEATER BOX

Booth knew *Our American Cousin* by heart. As a result, he knew that there would be a scene in the play when one actor stood alone on the stage. Booth planned to wait until the actor spoke a very funny line. At that moment, Booth would enter the box and shoot the president. Booth was certain that the audience's laughter would conceal the sound of his movements. In the confusion that would follow the shooting, he would jump from the theater box down to the stage. He would then escape through a door in the back of the theater. Booth was satisfied with his preparations, and believed his plan was complete. He left Ford's Theatre and returned to his hotel to eat supper.

This illustration of the theater box where President Lincoln would be seated shows the passageway and doors through which Booth would go to shoot the president.

As Booth worked through the afternoon, the Lincolns continued to make their evening plans. General Grant was visiting his children, and he politely refused the Lincolns' invitation. The Lincolns sent out several more invitations, but everyone they contacted was busy. Finally, a young Union officer, Major Henry Rathbone, and his fiancee, Clara Harris, accepted. The Lincolns left the White House and picked up the couple around 8:30 P.M. They arrived at the theater thirty minutes late.

Their entrance at Ford's Theatre brought the crowd to its feet. The play stopped and the orchestra struck up "Hail to the Chief" to announce the arrival of the president. Through the applause, Lincoln, his wife, and their two guests made their way into the private box and seated themselves. When the cheering finally faded, the play resumed.

Meanwhile, Booth met one final time with his conspirators. By then, Booth had learned that General Grant would not be at the theater. He quickly made new plans. Paine would attack the secretary of state, William Seward, who was resting in his home. Booth's friend, David Herold, would help Paine find the address. Atzerodt would carry out his plan to kill Vice President Johnson. By then, there could be no turning back. Booth had delivered a sealed letter to a local newspaper that afternoon.

David Herold

The letter listed his reasons for the assassinations. Booth signed it with his own name and those of his companions.

At 9:30 P.M., Booth rode his horse behind Ford's Theatre. Booth arrived earlier than he'd planned, so he entered a bar next to the theater and ordered a bottle of whiskey. As he drank, a man recognized Booth and said: "You'll never be the actor your father was."

"When I leave the stage," Booth answered, "I will be the most famous man in America."

11

Booth left the bar and entered the theater at 10:00 P.M. Inside the front lobby, Booth turned left and climbed the stairs leading to the second floor. Two actors were on stage playing out a scene. Booth quietly passed behind the seated audience and walked down the aisle toward the door that led to the president's box. Lincoln's guard sat in the audience. Booth located the man and received permission to enter the passageway. Only one actor remained onstage. Now was the time.

Booth opened the door and walked into the passageway. He picked up the wooden bar he

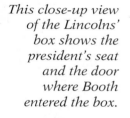

This close-up view of the Lincolns' box shows the president's seat and the door where Booth entered the box.

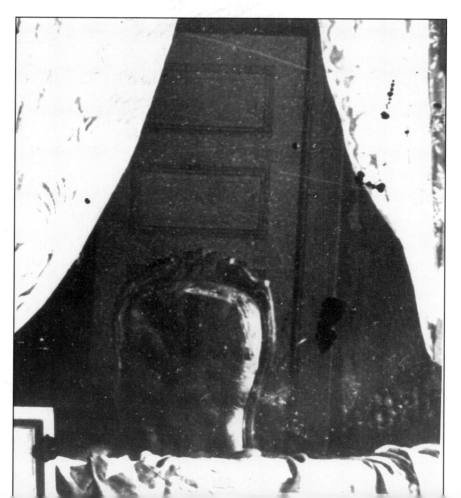

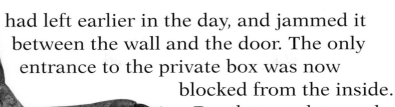

had left earlier in the day, and jammed it between the wall and the door. The only entrance to the private box was now blocked from the inside. Booth turned toward the only remaining door that separated him from the president. He peered through the hole he had drilled that afternoon. Inside the box, Lincoln sat gently rocking back and forth. Booth paused and put his ear to the hole. He waited for the line that would fill the theater with laughter.

Actor Harry Hawk stood alone on the stage, and the audience was enjoying his performance. Lincoln leaned forward in his chair to look toward the back of the theater. At that moment, Booth opened the door and entered the box. He stepped forward, the sound of his movements covered by the noise in the theater. He pulled the derringer from his pocket and held it behind the president's head. Below the theater box, Hawk recited the funniest line of the play: "you sockdologizing old mantrap." The audience roared with laughter. Booth pulled the trigger.

The sound of the gun's explosion filled the president's box and echoed onto the stage, startling Hawk into silence. Lincoln slumped forward as Mary turned in confusion. Behind her, Booth emerged from a cloud of gun smoke. Major Rathbone jumped from his seat and attacked the intruder. Booth faced the major and plunged his dagger toward Rathbone's chest. Desperately, Rathbone absorbed the blow with his arm and was knocked aside.

After Booth entered the theater box, (left) he managed to place the derringer within 6 inches (15 centimeters) of Lincoln's head before he fired.

After the shooting, Booth jumped down from the box to the stage, and escaped from the theater through a back door.

Booth scrambled to the railing of the private box and leaped to the stage 10 feet (3 meters) below. As he fell, his boot spur caught in a flag draped in front of the box. Booth landed awkwardly on his left leg, breaking it. He limped to the center of the stage and raised the bloody dagger to the shocked audience. "Sic semper tyrannis!," he cried. The Latin words were Virginia's state motto: "thus ever to tyrants!" Booth struggled off the stage and through a back door into the alley behind the theater. There, a boy patiently held Booth's horse, unaware of the events in the theater. Booth pushed the boy away and clumsily mounted the horse. Digging his spurs into the horse's side, rider and animal disappeared into the night.

Back inside the theater, Mary Lincoln's scream broke the stunned silence. Members of the audience turned to each other in confusion. Was this part of the play? Few had heard the gunshot over the laughter. Suddenly, Major Rathbone appeared at the box's railing and shouted: "Stop that man!" Mary Lincoln's wail sounded again, bringing the audience to its feet. "He has shot the president!," cried Rathbone. The theater exploded in chaos. Several people rushed to the theater-box door, but it was still blocked. Rathbone finally pried the bar loose and opened the door. Two young army doctors rushed to Lincoln's side. Mary Lincoln cried,

Dr. Charles Leale had graduated from medical school only two months before the night that Lincoln was shot.

"Oh, Doctor! Is he dead? Can he recover? Will you take charge of him? Oh, my dear husband! My dear husband!"

Twenty-three-year-old Dr. Charles Leale leaned over the unconscious president. Gently, he examined Lincoln's wound. The bullet had lodged in Lincoln's head, just behind his left ear. Leale knew immediately that the damage was serious. He rose to his feet and announced: "The wound is mortal. It is impossible for him to recover."

Leale wanted to move the president to the nearest bed to make him comfortable. Carefully, several soldiers lifted the president to their shoulders and carried him out of the theater. Groups of people looked on in shock and horror. Stepping out into the street, Leale scanned the darkened houses opposite Ford's Theatre wondering where to take the president. Suddenly, a man with a glowing lantern appeared on a front porch. "Bring him here!," he cried. The group slowly pushed through the crowd of onlookers and up the steps into the house.

Henry Safford

Today, the Petersen house is a national historic site.

The house was owned by a German immigrant named William Petersen. But Petersen was out in the city, celebrating the war's end. Henry Safford, the man with the lantern, had rented a room in the house. Dr. Leale turned to him, "Take me to your best room!," he ordered. Safford quickly obeyed. He led the group down a narrow hallway to a cramped bedroom in the rear of the house. There, they laid the president down on the bed.

William Seward sat for this photograph one year after he was stabbed by Lewis Paine. For the rest of Seward's life, he refused to allow the right side of his face, with its ugly knife scar, to be photographed.

Meanwhile, just a few blocks away, Lewis Paine and David Herold approached Secretary Seward's house. On the second floor, Seward was quietly dozing in bed. He had been in a serious riding accident a few weeks before. His right arm and jaw were fractured, making any movement sheer agony. His daughter, Fanny, and a young soldier sat quietly at his bedside. They hoped the secretary would enjoy a good night's rest.

While Herold waited out of sight in the darkness, Paine knocked on the front door of Seward's house. When a servant opened the door, Paine claimed that he had brought some medicine for Secretary Seward. The servant allowed Paine to enter the house and climb the stairs. On the second floor, Seward's son, Frederick, stopped him. Paine attacked Frederick, hitting him in the head with a pistol. Frederick collapsed. Paine rushed to Secretary Seward's bedroom, knocked open the door, and burst inside. He slashed the soldier with a knife and pushed aside Fanny. Paine jumped on the bed and began stabbing Seward in the face and neck. More members of the household rushed at Paine in frantic attempts to save Seward's life. Paine fled from the room and charged back down the staircase. He ran out into the street crying: "I am mad! I am mad!"

Back in the house, a servant leaned over Seward. The secretary opened his eyes. "I am not dead," he said. "Send for a surgeon, send for the police, close the house."

News of the night's deeds raced through Washington, spreading panic and confusion. Secretary of War, Edwin Stanton, was preparing for bed when he heard of the events. He rushed to the Petersen house. With both the president and the secretary of state unconscious, Stanton seized control of the government. He set up a small office in the Petersen parlor and interviewed witnesses. At first, Stanton believed that Confederate forces were attempting one last desperate bid for independence. After hearing several reports, however, Stanton realized that only a few men were behind the assassination attempts. He issued orders to find and capture John Wilkes Booth and his companions.

At about the same time, Lewis Paine was lost. David Herold had fled to join Booth, leaving Paine to find his own way out of Washington. Paine became confused on the dark streets of the city. He eventually wandered north and hid in a cluster of bushes.

George Atzerodt never got up the nerve to kill Vice President Johnson. Instead, he spent the evening walking from one bar to another. A few hours after midnight, Atzerodt rented a room at a boardinghouse and fell asleep.

Edwin Stanton worked through the night to find answers to the terrible events that had taken place.

Dr. Samuel Mudd

Throughout the night, government officials, doctors, family, and friends visited the dying president to say good-bye.

Booth easily escaped from the city. After leaving Ford's Theatre, he galloped south past the Capitol building and crossed a bridge into Maryland. Booth rode farther into the countryside for a few more hours before meeting up with David Herold. By then, Booth's broken leg was throbbing with pain. The two men stopped at Dr. Samuel Mudd's house to have the leg set. After splinting Booth's leg, Mudd invited Booth and Herold to spend the night. Exhausted from the night's events, they soon fell fast asleep.

In Washington, powerful officials, cabinet members, and doctors gathered at the Petersen house. Most of them crammed into the small

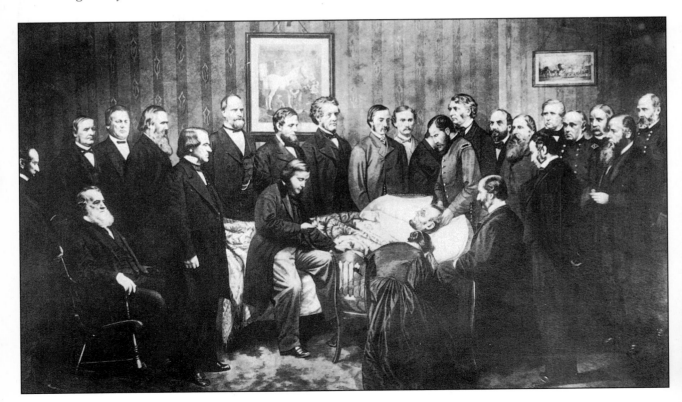

room where Lincoln lay unconscious. Dr. Leale sat at the president's side, checking Lincoln's pulse every few minutes. There was nothing anyone could do to save the president. In the next room, Mary Lincoln sobbed uncontrollably. Every few hours, she visited her husband's bedside and begged him to speak to her. In desperation, Mary called for their young son, Tad, insisting that Lincoln would speak to his own child. The president, however, showed no signs of waking.

This is the parlor where Mary Lincoln, joined by family members and Cabinet officers, awaited word about the president.

Through the night and into the early morning hours, the president clung to life. His breath came in gasps and his heartbeat grew weaker. Dr. Leale gently held the president's hand. If the president woke briefly, Leale wanted him to know that he was not alone. At 7:00 A.M., dawn began to light the room cheerlessly. Edwin Stanton joined the group and sat next to the president. At 7:22 A.M., April 15, Lincoln's chest heaved one last time and went still. Dr. Leale felt the last heartbeat in Lincoln's wrist before it, too, stopped. The room was silent. For several minutes, no one moved or spoke. Stanton finally raised his tear-soaked face to the ceiling and said: "Now he belongs to the ages."

This historic photograph of Lincoln's deathbed and bloody pillow was taken just a few minutes after the president's body was removed from the house.

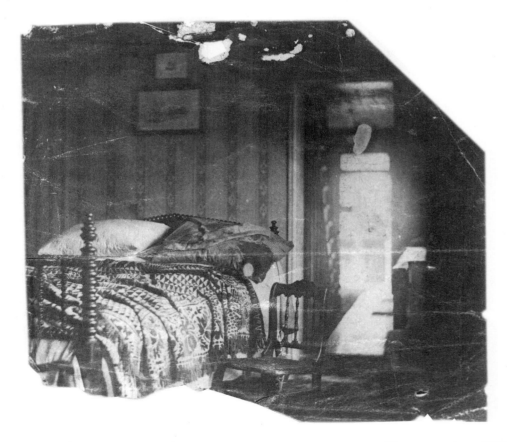

News of the president's death spread quickly throughout the nation and the world. Everywhere, newspaper headlines reported the tragedy. The mournful ring of church bells echoed through the cities and the countryside. Businesses shut down and people gathered in shock. They could not believe that the president was dead. An Illinois newspaper editor wrote: "He who writes this is weeping. He who reads it is weeping. . . . Hushed be the city. Hung be the heavens in black." Another newspaper reported: "mankind has lost its truest and best friend." An outcry was raised against the assassin, who still roamed free.

Buildings throughout Washington, D.C., including Ford's Theatre (the tall building on the left) were draped in black during the days following the assassination.

This "Wanted" poster that offered rewards for the capture of Booth and the conspirators stated, "Let the stain of innocent blood be removed from the land by the arrest and punishment of the murderers."

On April 21, Booth and Herold entered Virginia. For the past week, Union cavalry and police had been searching for Lincoln's assassin. Booth wrote in his diary: "I have been hunted like a dog through swamps and woods." Booth had expected to be welcomed throughout the South as a hero. Many southerners, however, thought Booth's actions were cowardly. Even southern newspapers criticized him.

After three more nights in hiding, Booth and Herold boarded a ferry to cross the Rappahannock River in Virginia. While on the ferry, Herold bragged to some passengers that he and Booth had assassinated the president. Three ex-Confederate soldiers heard their story and offered them shelter. Booth and Herold accepted. Their new companions took them to a tobacco barn near Port Royal, Virginia, that was owned by a farmer named Richard Garrett. A few hours later, Union cavalry tracked down one of the three soldiers and forced him to reveal Booth's location.

In the early morning darkness of April 26, Union cavalry surrounded the barn where Booth and Herold were asleep. The two men were startled awake by the noise outside. Herold quickly ran from the barn and surrendered. Booth, however, refused to come out.

The Union commander ordered that the barn be set on fire. Soon, the flames climbed the walls of the barn. Through slits in the barn wall, the soldiers watched Booth hobble frantically back and forth. One of the soldiers raised his gun and fired. The bullet slammed into Booth's neck, and he fell to the ground. Soldiers quickly entered the barn and dragged him to safety. Barely alive, Booth whispered to an officer: "Tell my mother I died for my country, and I did what I thought was best." He then asked that his hands be lifted to his face. Looking at them, Booth spoke his last words, "Useless. Useless." Lincoln's assassin was dead.

After being shot in the back of the head, soldiers dragged Booth from the burning barn. (Note Herold being held at gunpoint, right.)

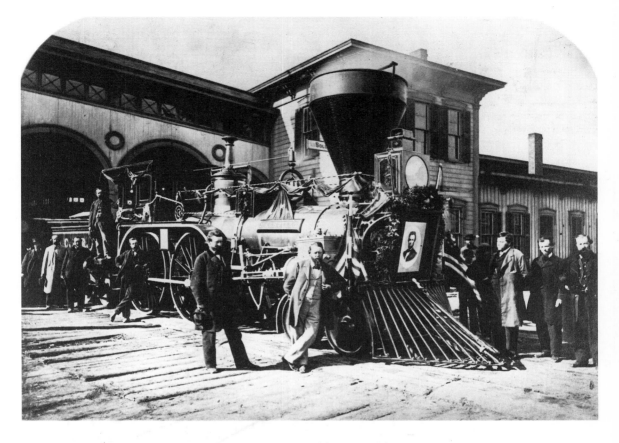

Booth's death offered little comfort to the grieving nation. Lincoln's body was placed on a train to make the journey back to his home in Springfield, Illinois. The funeral train wound slowly through the northern states. Citizens removed their hats respectfully as the train passed. In the cities where it stopped, thousands of people lined up to say a final good-bye to the president. On May 4, 1865, the train pulled into its final stop—Springfield. The president was laid to rest outside the city in Oak Ridge Cemetery.

Lincoln's funeral train was draped in black and carried a photograph of the president on the front of its engine.

After they were hanged, the bound and hooded bodies of (from left) Mary Surratt, Lewis Paine, David Herold, and George Atzerodt were removed for burial in nearby graves.

Mary Surratt was the first woman ever executed by the United States government.

During the next two months, several people stood trial for their role in Lincoln's assassination. Herold, Paine, Atzerodt, and a woman named Mary Surratt (the owner of the boardinghouse in Washington where Booth and his conspirators met) received death sentences. They were hanged on July 7, 1865. Three others, including Dr. Samuel Mudd, were sentenced to life imprisonment.

Today, Abraham Lincoln is remembered as one of the greatest presidents in the history of the United States. Lincoln ended slavery and guided the nation through its worst conflict—the Civil War. His speeches and letters reflect the ideals of freedom, government, and democracy on which the United States was founded. Today, Lincoln's words continue to inspire leaders and others throughout the world.

This is the only known photograph of Lincoln in death, taken as he lay in state in the Rotunda of the Capitol. Secretary Stanton refused to allow photographs of Lincoln's dead body, and ordered the destruction of this photo. It survived, however, but was lost until 1952, when a fifteen-year-old student discovered it while doing research about Lincoln.

GLOSSARY

agony – great pain or suffering

assassin – murderer of someone famous or important

cabinet – group of advisors for the head of a government

cavalry – soldiers who travel and fight on horseback

chaos – total confusion

conspirator – person involved in a secret, illegal plan

derringer – one-shot pistol with a short barrel that can be easily hidden in a pocket

ferry – small boat that carries passengers across rivers and lakes

immigrant – person who leaves one country to live permanently in another

mortal – something, such as a wound, that causes death

secede – to formally leave an organization or country

secretary of state – the top advisor in the president's cabinet

secretary of war – official who is responsible for directing the nation's war efforts

spur – pointed device attached to the heel of a boot

theater box – special section of seats that is set off from the rest of the seats in a theater; usually reserved for wealthy or important people

tyrant – ruler who siezes all of the power in a government

assassin

theater box

TIMELINE

November 6: Abraham Lincoln is elected president of the United States

December 20: South Carolina secedes from the Union

1860

1861 *April 12:* Fort Sumter is bombarded; American Civil War begins

1865 *March 17:* Booth's plan to kidnap President Lincoln fails

April 9: Confederate army surrenders; American Civil War ends

April 14: John Wilkes Booth shoots Lincoln; Lewis Paine attacks Secretary Seward

April 15: Lincoln dies

April 21–May 4: Lincoln's funeral train travels through northern states

April 26: Booth is cornered in a barn and killed

May 4: Lincoln is buried in Springfield, Illinois

July 7: Paine, Herold, Atzerodt, and Surratt are hanged

INDEX (*Boldface* page numbers indicate illustrations.)

PHOTO CREDITS

Photographs ©: The American Scene, Chicago, Illinois: 5 top, 28 top; Archive Photos: cover, 3, 7 top, 19, 20 bottom, 31 top; Corbis-Bettmann: 4, 6, 8 center, 8 top, 10, 11, 13 top, 14, 18, 20 top, 24, 26, 27, 30 bottom, 30 top, 31 bottom; Jay Mallin: 16; Meserve-Kunhardt Collection: 1, 2, 5 bottom, 7 bottom, 8 bottom, 12, 13 bottom, 17 top, 22, 28 bottom; North Wind Picture Archives: 15; Parks & History Association, Washington, D.C.: 17 bottom, 21; TJS Design: 9; UPI/Corbis-Bettmann: 23, 29.

ABOUT THE AUTHOR

Brendan January was born and raised in Pleasantville, New York. He attended Haverford College in Pennsylvania, where he earned his B.A. in History and English. An American history enthusiast, he has written several books for Children's Press, including *The Emancipation Proclamation, Fort Sumter, The Dred Scott Decision,* and *The Lincoln-Douglas Debates* (Cornerstones of Freedom). Mr. January divides his time between New York City and Danbury, Connecticut.